Children as Writers

Year 3

Written and illustrated
by Jim Edmiston

Acknowledgements:

Author: Jim Edmiston

Cover Design: Jim Edmiston and Kathryn Webster

The right of Jim Edmiston to be identified as the author of this publication has been asserted by him in accordance with the Copyright, Designs and Patents Act 1998.

HeadStart Primary Ltd
Elker Lane
Clitheroe
BB7 9HZ

T. 01200 423405
E. info@headstartprimary.com
www.headstartprimary.com

All rights reserved. No part of this publication may be reproduced, stored in a retrieval system, or transmitted in any form or by any means, electronic, mechanical, photocopying, recording or otherwise without the prior permission of the publisher.

Published by HeadStart Primary Ltd 2018 © **HeadStart Primary Ltd 2018**

A record for this book is available from the British Library -
ISBN: 978-1-908767-72-1

Year 3

CONTENTS

INTRODUCTION	2
FICTION	3
Familiar settings	5
Myths and fables	19
Fairytales and fantasy	27
Adventure and mystery	39
Science fiction and time-slip stories	49
Poetry and plays	59
NON-FICTION	67
Information and explanatory texts	69
Historical recounts and diaries	79
Newspaper reports	93
Instructions	99
PERSUASION	103
Advertising	105
Balanced arguments	109
Campaigns	115
Letters	119
PROOFREADING AND EDITING	123
Fiction	125
Non-fiction	131
Persuasion	139
FURTHER ASSESSMENT OPPORTUNITIES	143

INTRODUCTION

HeadStart Primary's *Children As Writers* contains no correct answers, only opportunities.

The intention is to strike a balance between supporting the teacher and providing opportunities for as many open-ended outcomes as possible. The exercises in this book encourage the child to go beyond their own expectations or wildest dreams – and, so often, writing is all about wildest dreams.

In most of the writing topics, there is an incremental movement through word, phrase and sentence work to something longer and more complete: like building a house. This isn't the same as starting a piece of fiction or non-fiction at the beginning and toiling your way through to the end. That isn't necessarily what writers do. They start with an idea, a character, a place, a prop, a conversation, a piece of intriguing information, at some point halfway through, or, if they're lucky, they have an ending already in mind.

In this series of books, the sections on fiction, non-fiction, persuasive writing and proofreading have been organised to follow closely the National Curriculum programme of study (at www.gov.uk) for writing skills:

> '...pupils should be taught how to plan, revise and evaluate their writing. These aspects of writing have been incorporated into the programmes of study for composition'.

Without the opportunity to proofread and edit their work, children are unlikely to reflect on the quality or effectiveness of their writing. They do this better – as we all do – if sufficient time has elapsed for them to have enough detachment to read what is on the page, rather than what they meant to put on the page. This is the reason for including a separate proofreading section, although, as a teacher, you will appreciate how important it is for children to work on their own writing, not just the practice pages provided here.

This last point is important and relates to the fact that the exercises in this book **should not be treated as worksheets** in the traditional sense. Ideally, the exercises should be used to provide enough stimulus and scaffolding to guide young writers towards a first draft. The teacher can then oversee the children's proofreading and editing, the resulting final version being completed in their writing book.

Examples of completed, edited writing can then be kept as evidence of an individual pupil's level of attainment, strengths and weaknesses, as well as year-on-year progress.

FICTION

familiar settings

myths and fables

fairytales and fantasy

adventure and mystery

science fiction and time-slip stories

poetry and plays

Familiar settings

National Curriculum references:

- create settings and plot in narratives
- organise paragraphs around a theme
- build a varied and rich vocabulary
- evaluate and edit
- proofread for spelling and punctuation errors

Feelings

How are these people feeling? If you can think of more than one word, write them all down.

More Feelings

Here are some more pictures of people.
How do you think they are feeling?

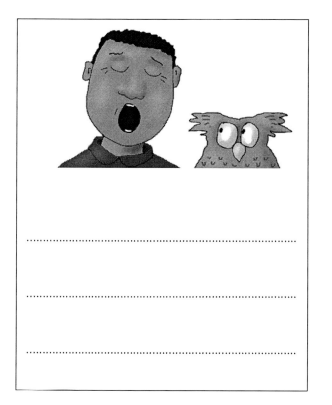

....

....

....

....

....

....

....

....

....

....

....

....

How Did I Feel?

The work you've done on words to do with **Feelings** will help you to complete these sentences.

When I won the egg and spoon race, I felt ....

When I ran off to school on Bank Holiday Monday by mistake, I felt ....

....

When I saw what my friend was having for lunch, I felt ....

....

When I realised I had lost my pocket money, I felt ....

because ....

When the owl suddenly hooted behind me, I felt ....

because ....

....

Build a Sentence

What Now?

Make up some more sentences about how you might feel when these things happen.

You won a prize you didn't expect.

You've been in the car for hours and you still haven't reached the theme park.

You are about to dive from the highest diving board for the first time.

Write a sentence about a time you felt very excited.

What Happened?

Choose one of your sentences. Create a story by writing a bit more about what happened.

One word often makes you think of another word. The second word might make you think of a third word and so on, like a trail of words.

Look at this example:

cat ⇒ mouse ⇒ cheese ⇒ sandwich

Create your own word trails, starting with these words:

jam ....

cake ....

boat ....

sky ....

foot ....

rain ....

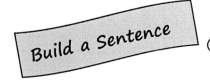

Build a Sentence — Word Pictures

Words can make pictures come into your head.
What do these words make you think of?
Write a sentence for each of these words.

circle

....

....

apple

....

....

robin

....

....

jelly

....

....

film

....

....

Build a Sentence  **MORE PICTURES**

Here are some words that might not go together very easily.
Write a sentence for each of these pairs of words.

| car monkey | .... |

....

....

| star puddle | .... |

....

....

| ice flower | .... |

....

....

| garden sock | .... |

....

....

Story Challenge

Write a short story about a **duck**, a **rainbow** and a **puddle**.

 **Word Work** Smiling Moon

Some things remind us of other things. Bees look like they're wearing striped shirts. Snow can look like icing on a cake. What do these things remind you of? They might remind you of more than one thing.

crescent moon: ....

....

....

digger: ....

....

....

skyscraper: ....

....

....

winding road: ....

....

....

What Is It?

How would you describe these things to someone who had never seen them before? Write a sentence for each one.

A dark forest

....

....

A firework display

....

....

A traffic jam

....

....

A stormy sea

....

....

A busy shopping centre

....

....

What Does It Look Like?

Write a short story that includes two of the following: a **winding road**, a **traffic jam**, a **busy shopping centre** and a **digger**. Give it a title.

What Does It Look Like?

Continue your story here.

Myths and fables

National Curriculum references:

- plan writing by discussing similar forms and learn from their structure
- create settings, character and plot in narratives
- organise paragraphs around a theme
- build a varied and rich vocabulary
- evaluate and edit

Magical Objects

Heroes and heroines in myths are often given a magical object with special powers that protects them. Here are some examples. Think up some of your own or make up new ones.

object	powers
magic carpet	flies across vast distances
crystal ball	sees into the future
unicorn horn	heals the sick and injured

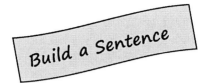

Mythical Beasts

Here are some creatures from ancient times that never existed but made story-telling very exciting. Write a description of each one.

Myths often describe what an amazing place the world is and the tasks involved in its creation. There are many different stories. Make up your own myths here. Describe where the following things come from. Are mythical gods, other worlds, journeys or magic involved?

special feature	myth – how did it come into the world?
fire	
rainbows	
trees	
sea	

The Greatest

Your hero or heroine is the greatest there has ever been. Picture them in your mind and answer these questions.

1. What is their name? ....

2. Where did they come from? ....

   ....

3. What special skills do they have? ....

   ....

   ....

4. What task have they been given? ....

   ....

   ....

5. Who has chosen them? ....

   ....

6. What is the special, magical object that will help them? ....

   ....

   ....

My Mythical Beast

Create your own mythical creature. Draw it, name it and describe it. What does it protect or stand guard over?

The Challenge

What happens when your hero or heroine meets your mythical beast? How is the magical object used? Is there a battle? Is the task achieved? Remember to give your story an exciting title.

The Challenge

Continue your mythical story here. Is there a surprise ending?

Fairytales and fantasy

National Curriculum references:

- plan writing by discussing similar forms and learn from their structure
- create settings and plot in narratives
- compose and rehearse sentences orally
- organise paragraphs around a theme
- build a varied and rich vocabulary
- evaluate and edit

FAIRYTALE FACES

Here are the faces of some characters from fairytales. Underneath, write down two or three words that describe them.

....

....

....

....

....

....

Try to imagine what these characters are thinking. Write their thoughts inside the bubbles.

Here are the other fairytale characters. What might they be thinking?

Write Time!

FAIRYTALE INTERVIEW

Imagine the Big Bad Wolf comes to your class one day and you interview him. What questions do you ask? What answers do you think he would give? You could work with a partner.

Me: Good morning, Mr Wolf. How are you today?

Mr Wolf: I'm very well, thank you.

Me: ....

....

....

....

....

....

....

....

....

Write Time!

This time, invite one of the other fairytale characters to come to your classroom. What questions would you ask? What answers do you think he or she would give? Again, you could work with a partner.

Me (interviewer): ....

Continue the interview here.

Fantastic Doors

Here are three doors to different fantasy worlds. Think of some words to describe them. Perhaps you could start by giving each door a name that makes it sound magical or mysterious.

Build a Sentence
Fantastic Doors

Imagine these three doors really exist. Make up some answers to the following questions:

> Where will you find each door?
> How do you open the door?
> What's behind the door?

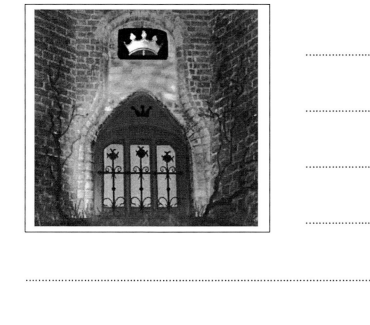

....

....

....

....

....

....

....

....

....

....

....

....

....

....

....

....

....

....

....

....

....

....

....

Fantastic Doors

Choose one of the doors. Imagine you have found it. What happens next?

Fantastic Doors

What is it like on the other side of the door? Who do you meet? How do you return? Continue your story here.

Adventure and mystery

National Curriculum references:

- plan writing by discussing similar forms and learn from their structure
- create settings and plot in narratives
- organise paragraphs around a theme
- build a varied and rich vocabulary
- evaluate and edit

 Word Work

My Camping Adventure

You are on a trail in the Rocky Mountains in Canada with camping equipment, food, water and a guide. But watch out for the bears.

Fill the gaps in the story using the words in the box.

| scared | path | listening | breathtaking | ready | binoculars |
| bellowing | tents | forest | lions | face | snuggled | snow |

Even though it was summer, _____ still lay on the high peaks. Earlier, our guide, Harriet, had pointed out the porcupine crossing our forest _____, and stopped us to listen to the _____ of a moose some way off.

The trail was long, but the _____ scenery helped me to forget how tired I was. All day I had my camera _____. I knew there were elk, wolves and occasional mountain _____ to be seen. Best of all, there were bears.

Once we had pitched our _____, we ate supper round the campfire, _____ to Harriet's advice. Maybe it was the dark. Maybe it was the secret noises in the _____ all around. Whatever it was, this was the moment I began to get _____.

Harriet reminded us that bears could be dangerous and were best seen through _____. She said that if you come _____ to face with one, talk quietly to it and, hopefully, it will ignore you. I crawled into my tent, _____ down into my sleeping bag and fell asleep, thinking about that word Harriet had used: 'hopefully'.

Then, in the middle of the night, ...

© Copyright HeadStart Primary Ltd

　My Camping Adventure

Look at the list of extra things you can take with you on your camping adventure. Choose five and say why they would be useful.

sunblock	first-aid kit	torch	spare batteries	extra map
chocolate	spare socks	matches	rubbish bags	compass

1. ....

   ....

2. ....

   ....

3. ....

   ....

4. ....

   ....

5. ....

   ....

My Camping Adventure

The camping adventure ended with the words: 'Then, in the middle of the night, ...' What happened? What noises are there outside your tent? Did some animal wander into the campsite? Finish the story here.

 **My Camping Adventure**

Continue the adventure story here.

 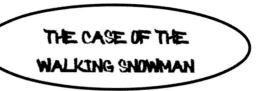

Make a word list of things to do with winter in this scene.

....

....

....

....

....

....

Build a Sentence — **WALKING SNOWMAN**

News reporters from around the world want to write about your mysterious snowman, who walked around while everyone was asleep. They fire question after question at you. What are your answers?

1. Describe the size of the snowflakes that night. ....

   ....

2. How deep was the snow around the house? ....

   ....

3. What clothes did you dress the snowman in? ....

   ....

4. Did your dad mind the snowman wearing his best scarf? ....

   ....

5. There was something unusual about the snowman. What was it? .

   ....

6. How can you be sure the snowman moved in the night? ....

   ....

7. What clues did the police discover? ....

   ....

WALKING SNOWMAN

What really happened? Write your story here.

> We stopped to admire the best snowman we had ever made. It was certainly the best dressed one we'd ever seen, with Grandpa's old army helmet, Dad's scarf, Grandma's golden buttons and Mum's boots.

WALKING SNOWMAN

Continue the mystery here.

Science fiction and time-slip stories

National Curriculum references:

- plan writing by discussing similar forms and learn from their structure
- create settings and plot in narratives
- organise paragraphs around a theme
- build a varied and rich vocabulary
- evaluate and edit

Alien Chat

Here are two aliens having a chat. Some of the words (**in bold**) look quite strange. What do you think they mean?

When I **kronked** off from my planet in my space **whizzer** this morning, the noise was so loud it gave me a terrible **branjab**. I'm getting fed up of invading Earth. The weather forecast says it'll be **diffle** tomorrow.

I know what you mean. When I **pronked** on Earth, I was totally **runkled**. I had to lie down for a quick **manj**. I was fine after a chocolate **smindelle**. I shouldn't **scramjam** too many of those. Bad for me.

alien word	meaning
kronked	
whizzer	
branjab	
diffle	
pronked	
runkled	
manj	
smindelle	
scramjam	

Nameless Superheroes

These superheroes need names that make them sound special. What names would you give them?

Build a Sentence

Super Powers

What powers do those superheroes have? It could be something unusual. Write a sentence for each one.

....

....

....

....

....

....

....

....

....

....

....

....

© Copyright HeadStart Primary Ltd

To the Rescue

Things couldn't get any worse. Pirates are going to throw you overboard into the shark-infested sea. Lightning is about to strike the ship. The captain's pet tiger has escaped from its cage. Luckily, one of the superheroes comes to your rescue. Which one? What happens?

To the Rescue

What's happening in your story? Try to think of an exciting ending.

Word Work

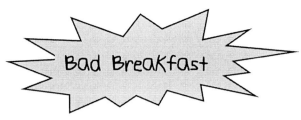

This is the start of a bad day when everything goes wrong. Underline the words, such as **tipped it over**, that describe what went wrong.

> What a morning! The first thing that went wrong was the porridge. It stuck to the saucepan. While I was trying to scrape it into my bowl, my dog, Fergie, ate my toast. I had forgotten to feed him. I didn't let the cat out either, so it decided to knock over the milk jug and lick the milk off the table. I couldn't find the marmalade until I sat on it and tipped it over. It spread all over my trousers. While I was wrestling Fergie to get what was left of my toast, I elbowed the butter onto the floor and slipped on it. I landed on my nose, scraped my knees and kicked the bin, sending rubbish all over the kitchen. I rushed out of the house, certain I would be late for school. I bumped into the postman. 'No school today,' he said. 'It's a holiday.'

Build a Sentence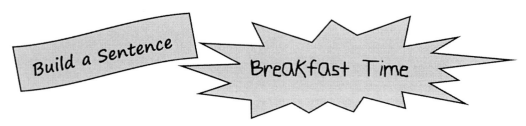

Breakfast Time

After you've had a good night's sleep, you wake up to find that you've gone back in time to yesterday morning when everything went wrong. Use the words in the boxes to write a sentence describing how you feel.

| dizzy |

....
....
....

| confused |

....
....
....

| incredible |

....
....
....

| speechless |

....
....
....

Now that you understand that you have gone back in time, this is your chance to make sure everything goes well. Look again at the order in which things went wrong. See what you can do to avoid the accidents and mistakes.

Breakfast Time

Continue your story about going back in time here.

Poetry and plays

National Curriculum references:

- plan writing by discussing similar forms and learn from their structure
- discuss and record ideas
- compose and rehearse sentences orally
- build a varied and rich vocabulary
- evaluate and edit
- read their own writing aloud to a group, using appropriate intonation and controlling the tone and volume so that the meaning is clear

Band Practice

Rhymes can often lead to ideas for a poem. Let's work on a poem about playing in a band. Add your own rhymes to those below.

instruments	other words
lute flute	toot parachute ....
	....
drum	strum chewing gum ....
	....
oboe piccolo banjo cello	throw bellow ....
	....
saxophone trombone xylophone	telephone groan ....
	....
guitar sitar	bizarre ....
fiddle	twiddle ....
recorder	disorder ....
double bass	instrument case outer space ....
	....
bassoon(s) spoons	balloons cartoons ....
	....

© Copyright HeadStart Primary Ltd

 ## Band Practice

Finish off these sentences, following the rhyming example shown.

> It's amazing how most of the audience **swoons** whenever Ronaldo plays hits on the **spoons**.

The audience feels there's something **bizarre** about ....
....

Cats and dogs all whine and **moan** when ....
....

Jennifer staggers all over the **place** ....
....

The next-door neighbour threw an old **boot** when ....
....

Grandma's cake collapsed in the **middle** when ....
....

Band Practice

It's time for your poem about a band. You could make some changes to your work so far or include other rhymes. If you think of any other rhymes, add them to the box before you put everything together.

tambourine – seen   bash – crash – clash   violin – mandolin
....
....

Having Great Grandpa over to stay the night isn't straightforward. This play needs some stage directions in brackets to tell the actors how to say their lines.

Title: **Great Grandpa's Sleepover**

Characters: NADIA, a girl aged 7 years. Her 93 year-old great grandpa, known as GRAMP. He is a bit hard of hearing.

Scene: kitchen in Nadia's house.

(Nadia is trying to persuade Gramp that it is his bedtime.)

NADIA: (………………………) Gramp, it really is time for your bed.

GRAMP: (………………………) No, Nadia. I don't want any more bread. I've eaten enough already. I need to go to bed.

NADIA: (………………………) That's just what … Oh, it doesn't matter.

GRAMP: (………………………) No, I don't want to get any fatter, but a mug of hot chocolate would help me go to sleep.

NADIA: (………………………) Ok, I'll make you some. Would you like a bedtime story as well?

GRAMP: (………………………) Hey! How about a bedtime story?

It's time to imagine the rest of Nadia's conversation with Gramp. Think of some answers to these questions.

1. What does Gramp say about the hot chocolate Nadia makes?

   ....

2. Once he's in bed, what kind of story does Gramp ask for?

   ....

3. Is there a part of the story that Gramp really enjoys?

   ....

   ....

4. What does Nadia think about the story? What does she say?

   ....

   ....

5. What does Gramp say as he's falling asleep?

   ....

   ....

Use your answers to the questions to write some more of the play.

Title: **Great Grandpa's Sleepover**

Characters: NADIA, a girl aged 7 years. Her 93 year-old great grandpa, known as GRAMP. He is a bit hard of hearing.

Scene: bedroom in Nadia's house. Nadia is holding a book. Gramp is tucked up in bed with a mug of hot chocolate.

(Nadia is hoping Gramp will fall asleep, but she is sleepy herself.)

....

....

....

....

....

....

....

....

If you need more space, you can finish writing the play here.

Title: **Great Grandpa's Sleepover**

Characters: ....

Scene: ....

....

(..)

....

....

....

....

....

....

....

....

NON-FICTION

information and explanatory texts

historical recounts and diaries

newspaper reports

instructions

Information and explanatory texts

National Curriculum references:

- plan writing by discussing similar forms and learn from their structure
- discuss and record ideas
- use simple organisational devices (e.g. headings and sub-headings)
- proofread for spelling and punctuation errors

Word Work

FROG FACTS

Here is a conversation about frogs. Underline the important facts.

Frogs in fairytales are usually green aren't they? But what about real frogs?

Our common frog is brownish yellow with dark blotches, so it's not easily seen by predators. That's called 'camouflage'.

Predators? Are those the animals that eat frogs? What are they?

Yes. Their predators include foxes, grass snakes, crows and ducks. Even your cat would eat a frog, if it found one.

And what do frogs eat? I suppose they must prey on other animals.

That's right. Frogs eat slugs and snails, worms and insects. When they're tadpoles, however, they're mainly vegetarian.

 **MORE FROG FACTS**

Here is some more information. Again, underline the important words.

I've seen frog spawn and we had tadpoles in our school pond.

Frog spawn can be found early in the year. Once the tadpoles emerge, they take about 12 weeks to lose their tail and grow legs.

Then they're like froglets, aren't they? Hopping around like tiny frogs.

Frogs have strong back legs that help them leap a long way and webbed feet for swimming quickly away from danger.

Do you think I might have any in my garden? Where should I look?

They like damp places. They hibernate under logs in winter or at the bottom of ponds, because they can breathe through their skin.

Frog Facts

Use the information to write a sentence for each of the following:

Appearance – what do they look like?

....

....

Movement – how do they move around?

....

....

Habitat – where do they live?

....

....

Food – what do they eat?

....

....

Predators – which other animals eat frogs?

....

....

Growth – how does a tadpole grow into a frog?

....

....

 **FROG POSTER**

Add information to this poster to make sense of the pictures. (If you enlarge this to A3 first, you'll have more space for your information.)

 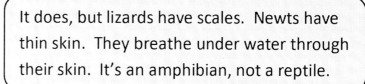 

Here is a conversation about newts.
Underline the important facts.

Is a newt a kind of lizard? In my book on animals, it looks like one.

It does, but lizards have scales. Newts have thin skin. They breathe under water through their skin. It's an amphibian, not a reptile.

I haven't seen a real one. How would I recognise one if I saw it?

The common newt is yellowish-green. In the mating season, the male gets more orange underneath and grows a crest along its back.

Frogs are amphibians too, aren't they. Do newts eat the same things as frogs?

Yes – slugs, snails and insects. Newt tadpoles eat water insects, and, sometimes, other tadpoles.

 **MORE NEWT NOTES**

Here is some more information. Again, underline the important facts.

Where would I be able to see a real newt? Do they live in ponds all the time?

Well, they live in woodland and meadows, but always near a pond. During the day they like to hide. They come out at night to hunt.

Maybe that's why I haven't seen one. What are they hiding from?

If they didn't hide during the day, they'd be eaten by blackbirds, grass snakes, rats, hedgehogs and a few other animals.

I forgot to ask how big they are. Do you get different kinds in this country?

The biggest and rarest is the great crested newt. It's about 15 cm long. The common newt is 10 cm and the palmate newt 7.5 cm.

 **NEWT NOTES**

Use the information to write sentences for each of the following:

Appearance – what do newts look like?

....

....

....

....

....

Habitat – where do they live?

....

....

....

Food – what do they eat?

....

....

....

Predators – which other animals eat newts?

....

....

 **NEWT POSTER**

Add information to this poster to make sense of the pictures. (If you enlarge this to A3 first, you'll have more space for your information.)

Historical recounts and diaries

National Curriculum references:

- plan writing by discussing similar forms and learn from their structure
- organise paragraphs around a theme
- use simple organisational devices (e.g. headings and sub-headings)
- evaluate and edit

THE SCHOOL FAIR

Here are some pictures of activities planned for the school fair. Think up a name for each one.

Build a Sentence

A GREAT DAY!

Imagine you were at the school fair. Finish off these sentences.

1. I helped at the school fair by ....
   ....

2. I tried the Lucky Dip and ....
   ....

3. The coconut shy was fun because ....
   ....

4. If you guessed the teddy's name correctly, ...
   ....

5. I won a box of chocolates when ....
   ....

6. The school will give all the money to a charity that ....
   ....

A GREAT DAY!

If you had been at the school fair, what sort of things would you have chosen to do? Describe the great time you had on this diary page.

NOT A GOOD DAY

What if you had a terrible time at the school fair? Describe the awful time you had on this diary page. What went wrong?

Medieval Mail

Here is some information about sending messages hundreds of years ago, when there were no phones, email or post. Fill in the gaps using the list of words inside the castle.

archers   deliver   weather   outlaws
hawks   weeks   write   message   secret

Long ago, not many people could read or ....

If they had to send a secret .... to someone, another person, called a scribe, would write it for them. Then, it wouldn't be a .... any more.

Riders taking messages would hope for fair .... and no .... Even the fastest messenger could take .... to .... the message.

Pigeons were also used, although they could also be caught by .... or shot down by ....

Pigeon Post

Sending news by carrier pigeon meant attaching a note to its leg, then letting it fly home, where the message could be read. It would have to be a few words only. Here is an example of a message being shortened. Try to do the other messages yourself.

Please send us all the soldiers you have available as quickly as possible. The castle is surrounded by our enemies. We won't last much longer.	**Castle attacked. Send soldiers.**
We don't have much food left. Some dry bread and one rotten apple are all that we have. We have only one barrel of water left.	
We have no arrows. Our archers have had no target practice. They fired all their arrows and didn't hit anything apart from a haystack.	
The king and queen have been up all night. The king is so tired he fell into the moat this morning and frightened the ducks.	
When our knights put on their heavy armour, they couldn't stand up. Then all their horses laughed and ran away.	
I hope you receive this message. Last time we sent out this pigeon, it flew off to the seaside for a couple of weeks. It came back with a tan.	

Pigeon Post

What might these notes mean? Write a sentence for each.

**Pigeon here.
No message.**

....
....

**Second pigeon.
Arrows sent.**

....
....

**Sorry – no
soldiers.**

....
....

**Food arriving in
4 wagons.**

....
....

**Minstrel sing
lullaby to king.**

....
....

Pigeon Post

The pigeon's messages show you the timing of events – how one thing happened after another. Write the complete story of what happened in the correct order. Think of a title.

Pigeon Post

Continue your story here. Remember it's your story, so you can add something unexpected if you like.

Build a Sentence — **All About Me**

What is your history? Write down some answers to these questions.

1. When were you born? ....

2. Where were you born? ....
   ....

3. Have you lived in different places? ....
   ....

4. Do you have younger / older brothers and sisters? ....
   ....

5. What happened on your first day at school? ....
   ....

6. Write down two special days that you remember and how old you were at the time.

   ....
   ....
   ....

Using the answers you have given, write the history of your life so far. You might like to add some more details to particular memories. Remember important facts to do with time, such as your age when things happened. Add your name to the title.

The History of ....

Continue writing your history here.

The History of ....

Newspaper reports

National Curriculum references:

- plan writing by discussing similar forms and learn from their structure
- organise paragraphs around a theme
- use simple organisational devices (e.g. headings and sub-headings)
- build a varied and rich vocabulary
- evaluate and edit
- proofread for spelling and punctuation errors

This shop window contains new hat fashions. The designers haven't given them special names yet. Think up your own names for them.

Build a Sentence

HATS! HATS! HATS!

As a newspaper reporter, you have interviewed some people wearing the new fashions. What did they say?

HAT NEWS

It's time to write your newspaper report. Describe some of the hats for your readers, and include some parts of your interviews. Also, start with an eye-catching headline and include a picture of a strange hat.

HAT NEWS

Continue your newspaper report here.

Instructions

National Curriculum references:

- plan writing by discussing similar forms and learn from their structure
- discuss and record ideas
- organise paragraphs around a theme
- build a varied and rich vocabulary
- assess the effectiveness of their own and others' writing and suggest improvements
- propose changes to grammar and vocabulary to improve consistency

Word Work — How to be a friendly person

Here are some children describing themselves. Under each one, note down something they might say or do.

People say I am very chatty.

....
....
....

I always try to be cheerful.

....
....
....

I do my best to be unselfish.

....
....
....

My friends say I am kind-hearted.

....
....
....

 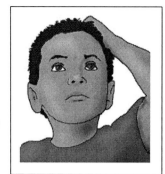

What if ...?

What would a friendly person do in these situations?
Write a sentence for each one.

1. A small girl drops her ice cream.

   ....

   ....

2. A friend's mother is struggling to put heavy shopping in her car.

   ....

   ....

3. Someone you know doesn't get any birthday cards.

   ....

   ....

4. Your best friend leaves their packed lunch at home.

   ....

   ....

5. Some of your friends won't let the new boy join in your game.

   ....

   ....

How to be a friendly person

It's time to write your instructions on how to be a friendly person. What should children do and what should they not do?

What to do	What not to do
....	....
....	....
....	....
....	....
....	....
....	....
....	....
....	....
....	....
....	....
....	....
....	....

PERSUASION

advertising

balanced arguments

campaigns

letters

Advertising

National Curriculum references:

- plan writing by discussing similar forms and learn from their structure
- discuss and record ideas
- organise paragraphs around a theme
- build a varied and rich vocabulary
- assess the effectiveness of their own and others' writing and suggest improvements
- propose changes to grammar and vocabulary to improve consistency

Word Work

The Birthday Company

What sort of things would be included in the best birthday party ever? Write down your ideas inside the balloons.

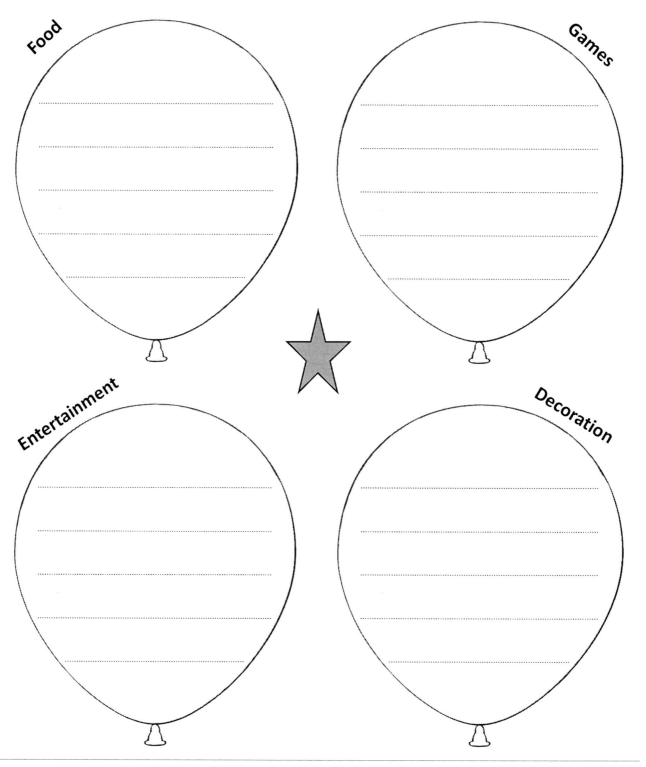

Build a Sentence — **The Birthday Company**

Imagine you are in charge of the Birthday Company – organising children's birthday parties. Tell your customers how great your parties are. Use some of the words in the gift box to describe them.

exciting unbelievable	lively delicious
breathtaking thrilling	brilliant colourful
magical fantastic	incredible enjoyable
amazing wonderful	spectacular outstanding
entertaining funny	pleasure delight
unforgettable special	treat surprise

Food

....

....

Games

....

....

Entertainment

....

....

Decoration

....

....

The Birthday Company

Design a leaflet for the Birthday Company, persuading people to let you plan their birthday parties. Include some of the words and sentences you've already used.

Balanced arguments

National Curriculum references:

- plan writing by discussing similar forms and learn from their structure
- organise paragraphs around a theme
- build a varied and rich vocabulary
- assess the effectiveness of their own and others' writing and suggest improvements
- propose changes to grammar and vocabulary to improve consistency
- read their own writing aloud to a group, using appropriate intonation and controlling the tone and volume so that meaning is clear

Make a list of games and activities to do in summer and another list for winter.

SUMMER and Winter

Finish these sentences:

1. When it's cold outside, I like to ....

   ....

2. On very hot days, I like to ....

   ....

3. I like the snow because ....

   ....

4. I don't like the snow when ....

   ....

5. When it's sunny in the garden, I like to ....

   ....

6. A day at the seaside is fun when ....

   ....

7. Staying indoors can be interesting if ....

   ....

Using the work you've already done comparing summer and winter activities, describe some of the things you like and don't like about playing in summer and winter. Give your writing a title.

SUMMER and Winter

Continue your writing here. Finish off by saying whether you like summer or winter the best.

Campaigns

National Curriculum references:

- plan writing by discussing similar forms and learn from their structure
- organise paragraphs around a theme
- build a varied and rich vocabulary
- assess the effectiveness of their own and others' writing and suggest improvements
- read their own writing aloud to a group, using appropriate intonation and controlling the tone and volume so that meaning is clear

Word Work

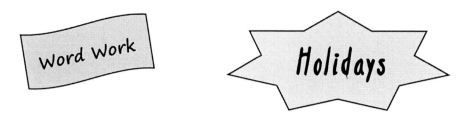

Write down words that come to mind when you think of holidays. They could be about how you feel as well as what you do during the holidays.

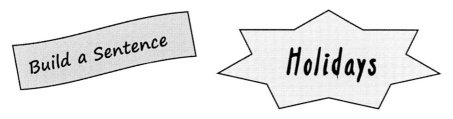

Build a Sentence — Holidays

Complete these sentences, persuading the government to give all children longer school holidays.

1. I would like longer summer holidays because ....
   ....

2. If I had longer holidays, I ....
   ....

3. I wouldn't get bored because ....
   ....

4. It's good to have a break from school because ....
   ....

5. When you are 7 or 8 years old, ...
   ....

6. Spending time in the open air is ....
   ....

7. What I would miss about school would be ....
   ....

No one would let you have longer holidays if they thought you were going to laze around, watching TV all day. You need good, persuasive reasons.

Why I Would Like Longer Holidays

....

....

....

....

....

....

....

....

....

....

Letters

National Curriculum references:

- plan writing by discussing similar forms and learn from their structure
- organise paragraphs around a theme
- build a varied and rich vocabulary
- assess the effectiveness of their own and others' writing and suggest improvements
- read their own writing aloud to a group, using appropriate intonation and controlling the tone and volume so that meaning is clear

You have had some special treats. They could have been planned by friends or members of your family. You decide. What words would describe these treats?

cake ....

....

ice cream ....

....

blockbuster film ....

....

games in the park ....

....

trip to a theme park ....

....

surprise present ....

....

a ride in a helicopter or hot air balloon ....

....

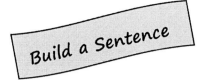 

Imagine you are telling a friend how wonderful those special treats were. Make each one sound like a very special experience.

1. ....

   ....

2. ....

   ....

3. ....

   ....

4. ....

   ....

5. ....

   ....

6. ....

   ....

7. ....

   ....

Write a friendly letter to the person who planned your special treats.

.... ← Write the date here.

Dear .... ,

....

....

....

....

....

....

....

....

.... ,

.... ← Write 'Lots of love' or 'Best wishes' and your name here.

PROOFREADING AND EDITING

fiction

non-fiction

persuasion

National Curriculum references:

- assess the effectiveness of their own and others' writing and suggest improvements
- propose changes to grammar and vocabulary to improve consistency
- evaluate and edit
- proofread for spelling and punctuation errors

Fiction

And Another Thing

The writer of this sentence has joined it all using the word *and*. Some of it could be separate sentences. Rewrite it so that it's easier to read.

> Mena and Mo spread their towels on the white sand and took their sandwiches out of their canvas bag and immediately ran down to the water's edge and dived in and, after splashing around in the bright sunshine, they spotted a nearby flock of birds swooping down and they were seagulls and Mena and Mo ran back to chase them away and stop them pecking at their sandwiches and then, suddenly, they heard a voice shouting "Help!" and they thought someone was drowning and it turned out that they had just been nipped by a crab.

Too Many Exciting, Gorgeous, Amazing Adjectives

Adjectives are useful for describing people, places and things, but too many can get in the way of the action. Can you improve this text?

> The enormous, hungry, fierce giant grumbled as he plunged from the twisty, winding, swaying beanstalk onto the hard, knobbly, bumpy ground. He made a loud, earth-shattering, ear-splitting groan as he spotted little, speedy, sneaky Jack running into the sweet shop. With long, bounding, thudding steps, the angry, furious giant followed. Shelves of delicious, smooth, creamy chocolate were knocked to one side as he approached Jack, waiting to be served by the cheerful, delightful, helpful assistant. Pushing Jack to one side, the giant bought one hundred shiny, colourful, attractive packets of ginger biscuits and climbed back up the beanstalk.

Past Mistakes

Because ancient myths and legends have been told and retold many times, they are usually written in the past tense. In the following sentences, the tenses of the verbs are mixed up and need correcting.

Long ago, Pandora will open the box and is letting out all the evil spirits into the world.

....

....

Theseus killed the Minotaur and is finding his way out of the maze because he followed the thread Ariadne will give him.

....

....

King Midas is feeling happy to turn things into gold, but when he had picked up his food, it will also turn into gold.

....

....

The monster called Medusa will turn people to stone if they looked at her, but Perseus will look at her reflection in his shield and defeated her..

....

....

The Wizard's Nightmare

Willard the Wizard has had a nightmare. He's written a note to his friend, Wez, about it. Still a bit sleepy, he's missed out some words. Rewrite it adding the missing words.

Dear Wez,

I had most awful dream last night. I was my kitchen and, instead of eating fish chips, I ate the dog's homework. The cat furious. The dog thought was huge joke. Then I washed face with toothpaste and brushed my teeth the frying pan. I dressed tortoise my pyjamas and went sleep in the dishwasher.

Then thought that I got up the next day, but was still part my dream.

I planned cycle the shops, but I noticed my bike square wheels. By time I walked supermarket they run out of muesli. I went home ate some dandelions instead. They disgusting!

I hope you well,

Willard

The Wizard's Nightmare

Rewrite Willard's note here, adding all the missing words, so that Wez has a better chance of understanding it.

Too Much Repetition

Some of these pronouns – *she, her, he, his, him, it, its, they, them* and *their* – could be very useful in replacing some of the repeated names of things and people in this short mystery.

> Maddy was sure they had taken a wrong turning. Maddy handed the map to Asif, who opened the map out and shone Asif's torch at it. Unfortunately, the torch's light was fading. The torch needed new batteries.
>
> Asif had to admit he and Maddy had been going around in circles for the past hour. Maddy and Asif's map of the castle was going to be of little help to Maddy and Asif.
>
> Once again, Maddy and Asif found themselves in the dungeon. The dungeon smelled foul, but this time things were worse. The dungeon's door slowly creaked and closed with an echoing thud.

Non-fiction

The Bare Bones

This page of information about the human skeleton has been printed without any punctuation. Read it carefully and add commas and full stops in the right places. Remember to add a capital letter after a full stop.

> The human skeleton grows as we grow up to become an adult an adult skeleton has 250 bones the largest one is the femur and the smallest bone is the stirrup which is inside the ear
>
> because the skeleton is rigid and strong it protects your heart lungs brain and other internal organs
>
> joints are where two or more bones join together such as at the knees elbows and fingers enabling us to bend
>
> muscles are attached to more than one bone so that when a muscle bulges and shortens it pulls the bone and allows us to move
>
> without a skeleton we wouldn't be able to stand up kick a ball scratch our nose or eat our lunch

Roaming Romans

These historical facts don't have a heading and are in no particular order, making it difficult to follow. Look at some information books to see how headings and sub-headings are used.

Roman soldiers had to be fit and strong enough to march as much as 20 miles each day in their heavy armour while carrying their weapons and equipment.

Roman soldiers were called 'legionnaires'.

The Roman Empire stretched from Britain across Europe to the Middle East and North Africa.

Women weren't allowed in the army.

Historians believe that the Roman Empire was so vast because the army was so well-trained and well-organised.

At the end of his fighting days, an old soldier would be given his own piece of land to farm.

Soldiers came not only from Rome but also other parts of the empire.

The soldier in command of a 'century' was called a 'centurion'.

A legion had between 4000 and 7000 soldiers.

Legionnaires patrolled the territories they had conquered and built bridges, roads and aqueducts, which were special bridges that carried water.

Each legion was divided into groups of 80 men. Such a group was called a 'century'.

Roaming Romans

Set out those facts about the Romans like a page from a history book with a heading and sub-headings.

Romans Still Roaming

Continue with your information page here. You could add a picture to make it more interesting for the reader.

How to Turn a Prince into a Frog

This recipe is confusing. Equipment and ingredients need to be in separate lists. The instructions would be easier to follow if they were numbered or had bullet points.

If you haven't got a hosepipe, go and borrow one. You'll have to dig a hole. Of course, you'll need a spade and a prince. Invite the prince around for afternoon tea. Collect lots of green vegetables, such as spinach and lettuce. That reminds me: you'll need some pond weed to put into the pond you are going to create in the garden. Remember to fill the hole with water first. Put the green vegetables, 100 ml of lime juice and 2 tablespoons of yoghurt into a blender and whizz together until it looks like a disgusting smoothie. I nearly forgot: put some water into your pond. Buy some special Magic Frog Powder from the witch who has a shop on Enchanted Lane. Add a teaspoon of the powder to the smoothie. (Beware! Adding too much could transform the prince into a large, green hippo.) Suggest to the prince that he might like to officially open your pond. So you'll need some scissors and ribbon for him to cut. Give him the smoothie to drink just before he cuts the ribbon.

How to Turn a Prince into a Frog

Write your equipment, list of ingredients and instructions here.

How to Turn a Prince into a Frog

Continue with your lists and instructions here.

Persuasion

Pet Adverts

Imagine some pets, looking for good homes, had put their own postcards in a shop window, advertising for owners. Everything about their writing would be wrong. See what you can do to correct them.

<u>freeee to a good home</u>
I a nice doggy doesn't eat chair legs chases car or howl during the night like go walks if not raining not bitey

<u>seeking new owner bring own perch</u>
polite parrot (never rude£ available goin cheap clean own sandpaper regular what you think? bargain?!?

<u>lovely boa constrictor like children</u>
quickly bee member of the family good for hugging and happy too do birthday parties not two squeezy just a bit when peckish

Pet Adverts

See what you can do to correct the pets' postcards.

Juggling with Prefixes

Prefixes such as *in*, *un*, *im* and *non* turn words into their opposites. It is important, however, to choose the right prefix. Correct this notice.

CIRCUS SKILLS

Do you think it would be **non**possible to learn tightrope walking? If you do, you would be **un**correct. It may sound **in**believable, but, after a few hours at Circus School, you could become an **im**credible circus star. **In**able to wait? Don't be **un**patient. Tomorrow, we will visit your school and show you how. There is no one who is **non**helpful or **in**friendly on our team. If the tightrope is **im**appealing, you can keep your feet on the ground and learn to juggle **un**stop with Katja the Clown.

Further Assessment Opportunities

Statutory guidance:

- A pupil's work in the subject being assessed alone may provide sufficient evidence to support that judgement, although evidence should ideally include work in other curriculum subjects.

- Teachers may consider a single example of a pupil's work to provide sufficient evidence for multiple statements.

- A pupil's work which demonstrates that they meet a standard is sufficient to show that they are working above preceding standards.

- A school's own tests, in addition to statutory tests, can be used as evidence to support a judgement. Furthermore, a pupil's answers to specific questions in any tests are acceptable forms of evidence to meet certain statements.

Assessment Opportunities: further notes

Teachers always need to keep an eye on children's progress, on strengths and weaknesses, in order to plan next steps. Writing is judged in terms of how well structurally, grammatically and compositionally it achieves the writer's aim to describe, to inform, to explain, to persuade or to entertain.

Teachers are expected to base their judgements on 'a broad range of evidence from across the curriculum for each pupil'. Also, 'individual pieces of work should be assessed according to a school's assessment policy'.

Further guidance can be found here:

https://www.gov.uk/government/publications/2018-teacher-assessment-exemplification-ks2-english-writing

Copies of the teacher exemplification materials are also available on the CD-ROM which accompanies this book. These further assessment opportunities are provided to help the teacher build up a body of evidence of an individual pupil's responses to a range of writing challenges. They are intended to be used by teachers as an extra tool to support their professional judgement.

The first page, entitled English Writing Key Stage 2 (for recording name, class, date and record of achievement), is printed here only once and should be treated as a master page to be photocopied for each writing session.

Recording levels of achievement in the table provided is a matter of assessing whether a child is:
- working towards the expected standard
- working at the expected standard or
- working at greater depth within the expected standard.

Individual pieces of written work are only a guide to achievement and progress and should be used in conjunction with ongoing teacher assessment.

Fiction and non-fiction are included, as well as shorter and longer tasks. In the past, pupils were allowed 20 minutes for shorter writing tasks and 45 minutes for long writing tasks. Teachers should make their own judgement in line with the school's established assessment practice.

Planning is a skill in itself. It would be beneficial if teachers were to model the planning process, emphasising that this preliminary stage is about getting down on paper some quick notes. This is not an exercise in elegant handwriting or extended prose. This is a time for key words, an interesting phrase or two, a list or a quick timeline. It is not the time to stop and try to polish the writing.

English Writing

Key Stage 2

NAME	
CLASS	
DATE	

Your teacher will read through the task and explain how long you have to plan and complete each piece of writing. Drawings and decoration are not part of this writing task.

Task	Title	Achievement
Short writing		
Long writing		

Overall achievement	Notes

SHORT WRITING TASK

The Animal I Would Be

What if you were born, not as a human, but as some other sort of animal? What would that be like?

> **Your task is to describe what sort of animal you would be and give reasons for choosing it.**

PLANNING NOTES

What sort of animal?	
Reason 1	
Reason 2	
Reason 3	

The Animal I Would Be   My name: _____

LONG WRITING TASK

Spending a Million

It might be exciting having a million pounds to spend. Would you spend it all on yourself? Would you buy special treats for your friends? Would you use it help other people?

> **Your task is to describe what you would do with all that money and say why.**

PLANNING NOTES

Choice 1	
Reason	
Choice 2	
Reason	
Choice 3	
Reason	

Spending a Million

My name: _____

Spending a Million

My name: _____

SHORT WRITING TASK

Talking Pet

What would it be like if you had a pet that could talk? What do you think it would say to you? What sort of things would you chat to it about?

Your task is to decide what kind of pet you have in mind. What would a conversation with it be like?

PLANNING NOTES

What type of pet is it?	
What might you talk about?	

Talking Pet

My name: _____

LONG WRITING TASK

Toy's Adventure

You leave your favourite toy on the bus. What adventures happen to it?

> Your task is to describe the different things that happen to your toy. Does it find its way back home?

PLANNING NOTES

Who are the people who play with the toy?	
Where does it go?	
What happens to it?	
Does it return home?	

Toy's Adventure

My name: _____

Toy's Adventure

My name: _____

SHORT WRITING TASK

A Fantastic Tale

Think of the best fantasy story you have read, seen on television or at the cinema. What was so good about it – the characters, the setting, the special effects on screen or the pictures it created inside your head?

> Your task is to describe the main things you enjoyed about the fantasy. Explain why it was better than other fantasies.

PLANNING NOTES

What is the title of the fantasy?	
What special characters were in the story? What did they do?	
What other things made it special?	

A Fantastic Tale

My name: _____

| LONG WRITING TASK |

Party Instructions

You have been put in charge of the class Christmas party. You don't have to do all the work yourself, but you do have to write out instructions for all your helpers.

> Your task is to make a list of food and equipment, as well as write clear instructions to ensure everyone has fun at the party.

PLANNING NOTES

What equipment will be needed?	
What food and prizes will there be?	
What other things will there be to do?	

Party Instructions

My name: _____

Party Instructions

My name: _____

SHORT WRITING TASK

My Favourite Lessons

Children have been given Friday afternoons to spend more time on their favourite lessons. You can choose one or more subjects.

> **Your task is to persuade your headteacher to give you more time to work on your favourite lessons.**

PLANNING NOTES

Favourite lesson 1	
Favourite lesson 2	
What will you say that might persuade your teacher to give you more time on your favourite lessons?	

© Copyright HeadStart Primary Ltd

My Favourite Lessons

My name: _____

LONG WRITING TASK

Newsflash!

A strange, pyramid-shaped flying machine has landed nearby. Some people saw it arrive. A robot, the height of a double-decker bus, is standing beside it. The police are keeping people back.

> **Your task is to visit the place where the alien craft has landed, get as much information as you can and write a newspaper report.**

PLANNING NOTES

Describe the flying machine.	
Describe the robot.	
What was seen and who saw it?	

Newsflash!

My name: _____

Newsflash!

My name: _____

SHORT WRITING TASK

What Would I Do?

Imagine you were stranded out at sea on a small lifeboat. You have some food and drinking water. What would you do to survive until you were rescued?

> **Your task is to describe how you would pass the time, keep up your spirits and survive until the rescue helicopter picks you up.**

PLANNING NOTES

What would you do about eating and drinking?	
How would you pass the time?	
How would you keep your spirits up?	

What Would I Do?

My name: _____

LONG WRITING TASK

Then What?

> The light was fading. An angry storm was about to break. The cave was my only hope of staying dry and safe till morning. I was so relieved to stumble inside just as the rain and whipping wind reached me. Moments later, a strange sound came from deep within the darkness of the cave.

Your task is to think about the strange sound and continue the story.

PLANNING NOTES

What is the strange sound?	
What happens?	
How does it end?	

Then What?

My name: _____

Then What?

My name: _____

SHORT WRITING TASK

Litter Letter

A letter of complaint needs to be sent to the local council, who don't know that a grassy playing area is being covered in litter, plastic bottles and broken glass.

> Your task is to use persuasive words and phrases in a letter convincing the council to clean up a play area.

PLANNING NOTES

What's wrong with the playing area?	
What words and phrases would persuade the council?	

Litter Letter

My name: _____

LONG WRITING TASK

The Perfect Town

Towns are not just buildings and roads. Some have parks; some are on the edge of the countryside. All of them are full of people working, playing and going to school.

> Your task is to describe what you think the perfect town would be. What would it be like to live there?

PLANNING NOTES

Where would the perfect town be?	
Describe the buildings.	
What other ideas do you have?	

© Copyright HeadStart Primary Ltd

The Perfect Town

My name: _____

The Perfect Town

My name: _____